Giant Animals

Einstein Sisters

KidsWorld

The **blue whale** is the **biggest** animal that has ever existed, even bigger than the dinosaurs. It can be up to **100 metres long,** the length of 2 Olympic swimming pools. It can weigh more than **180 tonnes.**

Blue Whale

Biggest Animal!

This whale is also one of the loudest animals on the planet. Its rumbling call is louder than a jet! The call can be heard for many kilometres under the water. The whale calls to "talk" to other blue whales.

This whale grows so large by eating one of the smallest animals on the planet—krill.

Biggest Land Animal!

African Elephant

Farmers in Kenya use **beehives** to keep **hungry elephants** away from their **crops.** If the elephant **bumps** the fence around the farm, the beehive **shakes** and **angry bees** fly out. They **chase** the elephant away.

There are **two types** of elephant—the **African** and the **Asian** elephant. The African elephant is the **biggest land animal** in the world. It can grow **twice as tall as a man** and **weight** more than **75 men.**

Elephants **sleep** for only **5 or 6 hours** a day. They can sleep standing up, **leaning against a tree** or lying down.

The elephant's **closest living relative** isn't the rhino or the hippo— it's the **rock hyrax.** The rock hyrax is about the size of a rabbit.

Giraffe

Giraffes are the **tallest animals** in the world. They can be up to **6 metres** tall, about as tall as a **2-storey house!** Their legs are so **long** that most women could walk right under a **giraffe's belly** without **ducking.**

Giraffes live in Africa in **small groups.** Giraffes usually **get along** with each other, but sometimes the males, called **bulls,** fight. Fighting bulls **whack** each other with their **strong neck** until one gives up and **walks away.**

Because they are so **tall**, giraffes can **eat** the leaves at the **tops of trees**, way out of reach of other **leaf-eating** animals. They really like the **leaves and buds** of **acacia trees**.

Tallest Land Animal!

Biggest Fish!

The whale shark is the **world's** biggest fish. It can grow to more than **12** metres long, longer than a **school** bus. It weighs about **34** tonnes.

Whale Shark

The whale shark lives in tropical waters. It is a favourite of scuba divers because it is so friendly.

The whale shark has about 3000 tiny teeth. No one is sure what it uses them for. Filter feeders don't really need teeth.

Every whale shark has its own pattern of yellow spots on its skin.

This huge shark is a filter feeder. It eats plankton, krill and small fish. To catch its food, the shark swims with its mouth open. It sucks up water then pushes it out through its gills. Special parts on the gills, called gill rakers, trap the food as the water passes through the gills. The shark then swallows the food that is left behind once all the water is gone.

Biggest Ray!

This ray is a **filter feeder**. It **eats** small fish, plankton and **krill**. It has **no teeth**.

When it **swims**, the manta ray looks like it is **flying underwater**. It flaps its **"wings,"** which are actually **dorsal fins**. This huge ray can even **leap** out of the water.

The manta ray can grow to more than 7.5 metres long, almost the length of **2 cars.** It is closely related to **sharks.**

This ray lives in tropical waters. It can usually be found around **coral reefs.**

The manta ray visits "cleaning stations" where other smaller fish, like angelfish, **clean** its body and gills of **parasites.**

Manta Ray

Biggest Anteater!

Giant Anteater

This anteater can **grow** to be **bigger** than a German shepherd.

The **giant** anteater **has no teeth.** Its stomach **grinds** up its food. Along with **ants** and **termites,** this anteater will also eat **ripe fruit** it finds on the **ground,** as long as the fruit is small enough to fit in its **tiny mouth.**

The **giant** anteater can stick its tongue out **60 centimetres,** about the length of a **tennis racket,** to catch ants or **termites.**

This anteater's claws are longer than **human fingers.** The anteater uses its claws to tear open ant hills and termite mounds. It then uses its **sticky tongue** to slurp up its prey. It can only **stay** at each mound for **1 minute** or so because ants and termites will **sting** to defend **their nests.**

Goliath Bird-eater Spider

The **Goliath bird-eater spider** is the world's **biggest** spider. It is about the size of a man's hand. The **giant huntsman spider** has longer legs, but the **bird-eater is heavier.**

When this spider is **scared,** it makes a **hissing noise** by **rubbing** the hairs on its **legs together.**

This spider likes **marshy** or **swampy** areas in the rainforests of **South America.** It lives in a **burrow** in the ground.

Females live for **12 to 15 years**. Males live only for **3 to 6 years**.

Biggest Spider!

This spider eats mostly **bugs**. It will also eat **rodents**, frogs, toads, lizards and **snakes**. It doesn't usually eat birds.

Biggest Tree-living Animal!

When it rains, orangutans make **umbrellas** out of **big leaves** to keep dry.

Orangutans **eat** mostly fruit. They will also eat **leaves**, **flowers** and insects.

Orangutan

The orangutan can move around on the ground but spends most of its time in the trees. It even **builds a nest** in a tree **for sleeping.**

Orangutans are a type of **ape.** They live only in the **rainforests** of **Borneo** and **Sumatra.** Logging in these forest is **wrecking** the orangutans' habitat. They are now **endangered,** which means that there are not many left in the world.

A liger named **Hercules** holds the record as the **world's biggest cat.** He is more than 1.8 metres tall and 3.5 metres long. When he stands on his back legs, his paws can reach the top of a **double-decker bus!**

Ligers are a cross between a **lion father** and a **tiger mother.** They are the **biggest** cats in the world. **Tigons,** a cross between a tiger father and a lion mother **also exist** but are **much smaller. Ligers** and **tigons** do not exist in the wild. Lions and tigers do not get along in nature.

The **Siberian tiger** is the biggest cat **in the wild.** It can grow to be about 3.5 metres **long,** almost the length of a **car.**

Biggest Cat!

Liger

Giant

This otter lives in only 3 river systems in South America. Its main food is **fish**, but it will also eat **crabs, snakes** and even small **caimans.**

At 1.8 metres long the **giant otter** is the **biggest** member of the **weasel family.** It is also the **rarest.** There are only a **few thousand** left in the **wild.**

Giant otters live in **small family groups.** Baby otters, called **cubs**, stay with their family until they are about **3 years old.** Cubs are born completely **covered in fur**, even their nose!

Goliath Beetle

Not only is the goliath beetle the **biggest beetle,** it is one of the **biggest insects** in the world. It can grow to be the size of a **man's palm.**

These **giants** have **two sets of wings.** The first pair, called the **elytra,** protect the second pair, which are used **for flying.**

This **beetle** can **lift** things that are **850 times** heavier than itself.

There are **5 species** of goliath beetle. They all live in **Africa**.

Biggest Beetle!

Biggest Rodent!

The capybara is the **world's biggest rodent.** It grows to around **60 centimetres tall,** about the same as a **German shepherd.** It lives in **South America.**

Capybaras **love water.** They live around rivers, streams, lakes and ponds. When there is **danger,** capybaras will **hide underwater.** They can **hold their breath** for up to 5 minutes.

Capybara

The Capybara has **webbed feet**. It is a **good swimmer** and can also **walk** underwater.

Its **ears, nostrils and eyes** are on the top of its head. This way the capybara can keep most of its body **underwater** but still **breathe** and **see** above the water.

Its scientific name means "**water hog**" because people used to think it was a kind of **pig**.

Biggest
Primate!

Gorillas are the **biggest** primates **in the world.** Males are **larger** than females. A full-grown male **gorilla** can be as **tall** as a man and can weigh as much as **2 men.**

They **sleep in nests** that they build on the **ground** or low in **trees.** The nest are made of **leaves and branches.** They do not **reuse** old nests but make a new one **every night.** Baby gorillas share their mom's **nest.**

Baby gorillas need their **mom** to take care of them until they are about **3 years old.**

Gorilla

Ocean Sunfish

The ocean sunfish is also called a **mola.** Its favourite food is **jellyfish.**

The ocean sunfish is the world's biggest **bony fish.** It can grow to more than **4 metres high,** bigger than a car. It weighs around **2 tonnes.** Some sharks are bigger, but they are not bony fish. Bony fish have a **skeleton** made of **bone.** A shark's skeleton is made of **cartilage.**

This sunfish looks like a giant fish head with fins. It has no real tail, just a **bumpy** stump called a **clavus.** To swim it has to use the fins on the top and bottom of its body. It has no scales, just **rubbery** skin.

Biggest Bony Fish!

Female **ocean sunfish** lay up to 1 million eggs, more than any other **fish.**

Biggest Monkey!

Mandrill

The **mandrill** is the **world's biggest monkey**. It is almost the size of a **German shepherd** but **weighs** half as much. It lives in rainforests in **Africa**.

It is also the most colourful primate. The **male** has bright **white**, **red** and sometimes **blue skin** on its face, a yellow **beard** and a colourful **bottom**. The female is smaller and less **colourful** than the male.

Mandrills eat mostly **fruit** and other **plant matter**, but they will also eat **insects**, reptiles, birds and small **mammals**.

These **monkeys** spend most of their **day** on the ground but **sleep in trees**.

Biggest Moth!

Atlas Moth

The Atlas moth is the **biggest moth** in the world. It is bigger than a **dinner plate!**

This moth **has no mouth**, so it **does not eat**. It has to rely on the stores it built up when it was a **caterpillar**. It usually only lives for about **2 weeks** as a **moth**.

This moth's wingtips look like snake heads.

It is easy to tell **male** atlas moths from **females**. Male moths have **feathery antennae** and are smaller than females.

Atlas moth **caterpillars** are **blueish green** and have a white **powdery** coating. They stay in their **cocoons** for about **4 weeks** before coming out as a **moth**.

Ostrich

The **male ostrich** has **black feathers** with a bit of white on his wings. The **female's** feathers are more **brownish grey.**

The **ostrich** is the **biggest**, heaviest bird **in the world.** It is taller and **weighs** more than twice as much as a **man.** Because it is so heavy, **it cannot fly.**

Ostriches only have **2 toes.** Other birds have **3 or 4.**

The **ostrich** also lays the **biggest egg.** An ostrich egg can weigh as much as **24 chicken eggs!** Ostrich **chicks** are about the size of an **adult chicken** when they are **born.**

Biggest
Bird!

Biggest Centipede!

Giant Centipede

The **giant centipede** is also called the **Peruvian giant yellowleg**. It is the **biggest centipede** in the world. It can grow to be about as **long** as your **ruler**.

These beasts **eat mostly bugs**. They can also eat mice, lizards, frogs and **small birds**. Some giant centipedes in Venezuela **hang** from the ceiling of the cave and **eat bats!**

Some people keep these centipedes **as pets**.

Giant centipedes live South America. They like tropical and sub-tropical **forests**.

These centipedes have **a poisonous bite**. Their **poison is strong** enough to make a person sick.

Gaur

Both **male** and **female** gaur have horns.

The **gaur** is the biggest **bovine** in the **world**. It is also the fourth **biggest land animal.** Only the elephant, rhino and hippo are **bigger.**

It is also called the **Indian bison** and the **seladang.** It lives in Asia in **herds.** Each herd is led by a female, called the **matriarch.**

Because they are **so big,** gaur only have **2** natural predators—the **tiger** and the saltwater crocodile. When faced with a tiger, **gaur** will form a circle around their **calves** or weak members of **the herd.**

Biggest Bovine!

The **gaur** is usually **active during the day**, but in places where **people live** too close to its **habitat**, it has become **active at night**.

Biggest Seal!

Male and female **elephant seals** do not eat the **same prey**. Females eat mostly **squid**, and males eat squid, **fish**, crabs, rays and small **sharks**.

The southern elephant seal is the **biggest seal** in the world. A male grows to be **way bigger** than a **car** and can weigh more than **4000 kilograms**, more than 50 times as much as a man. **Female** elephant seals are much **smaller** than males.

Southern Elephant Seal

This huge seal can **hold its breath** underwater for almost **2 hours.**

The **elephant seal** gets its name for the male's huge nose, called a **proboscis.** The proboscis starts to grow when the male is about 4 years old. He uses it to **make loud roars** when he is fighting **other males.**

Biggest Flying Bird!

Condors eat dead animals that they find. They don't usually hunt for themselves, but they will steal eggs and even baby birds out of nests.

The **Andean condor** is a type of vulture. It is considered the **biggest** bird that can **fly.** From wingtip to wingtip, this condor reaches more than **3 metres,** about the length of a **small car.**

The condor has **no feathers** on its **head** so it won't get covered in **gunk** as it eats rotting meat. The bodies it feeds on are often quite messy by the time the condor gets to them.

The **kori bustard** is another of the world's **biggest flying birds,** not for its wingspan but for its **weight.** This **bustard** weighs about as much as a 4-year-old child.

Bullet Ant

Biggest Ant!

This ant's favourite food is **nectar,** but it will also eat **fruit** and **insects.**

The **bullet ant** the world's **biggest ant.** It grows to be about the length of an **almond.** It lives in the **rainforests** in **Central America.**

This ant has the most **painful sting** of any animal. People who have been **stung** compare it to being **hit by a bullet,** which is **how** the ant got its name.

It is also known as the **conga ant,** the **lesser giant hunting ant** and the **24-hour ant** (because that's how long the **pain of its sting** lasts).

Kakapo

The **kakapo** is the world's **biggest parrot**. It weighs about as much as a **house cat**. Though the **hyacinth macaw** is longer from beak to tail, the kakapo **weighs** almost **twice as much**. This bird can live to be more than **100 years old**.

The kakapo is considered **critically endangered**. There are less than **150 left** in the wild. They live on 3 islands in **New Zealand** that are kept **free** of **cats**, **weasels** and other **animals** that would **kill them**.

Biggest Parrot!

The kakapo is the only flightless parrot. It climbs trees to get to its favourite food, fruit. It also jogs along the forest floor to get to feeding sites.

Giant African Land Snail

These giant snails **never stop growing.** They **grow quickly** for their first 6 months, then grow **really slowly** for the rest of their lives. They can live for up to **10 years,** though most only live **5 or 6.**

Giant African land snails do not have **teeth.** They have a rough tongue, called a **radula,** that lets them **scrape food** into their mouth.

Giant African land snails are the **biggest snails** in the **world.** They grow to be about the size of **this book.**

Biggest Snail!

Because they are **so big,** these snails have **no natural predators.**

Females lay their **eggs** 5 or 6 times a year. They can lay up to **200 eggs** at a time!

Biggest Bat!

Flying foxes are the **biggest bats** in the world. They are the size of a **fox.** There are **many** different species. They live in **Australia** and **southeast Asia.**

Some types of **flying fox** eat mostly **fruit**, and others eat mostly nectar and pollen. The nectar eaters help **pollinate plants**, much like honeybees do.

Flying foxes do not have echolocation. Instead they have **great** eyesight, even in the **dark.**

Flying Fox

Anaconda

Biggest Snake!

The **green anaconda** can grow longer than **2 mini vans** and weigh as much as **3 men**. It lives in **swamps**, streams and marshes in **South America**.

The anaconda gives birth to **live babies** instead of **eggs**. The female usually has between **20 and 40 babies** at a time.

Because it is so **heavy**, the **anaconda** moves much easier in the **water** than it does on **land**.

Its eyes and nostrils are on **top of its head** so it can keep them **out** of the water as it **swims**.

There are **4 species** of anaconda: the **green**, the **yellow**, the Bolivian and the darkly-spotted anaconda. The green anaconda is **biggest** species.

Biggest Tortoise!

This tortoise can **live** for up to a year **without food or water.**

Lonesome George is the most **famous** Galápagos tortoise. He was a **Pinta Island tortoise** and for many years was the **last of his kind.** He died in **July 2012,** so the Pinta Island tortoise is now **extinct.**

The Galápagos tortoise is the biggest tortoise in the world. It is also one of the most **long-lived creatures,** usually living more than **100** years.

This tortoise lives on **7** of the **Galápagos Islands,** west of **Ecuador.** There once were 15 species of Galápagos tortoises; now there are only **11,** and they are all endangered.

Galápagos Tortoise

Biggest Penguin!

To **move** about on land, the **emperor penguin** often **waddles.** It may look awkward, but for short distances this penguin can waddle **as fast as a human can run.** The penguin will also **toboggan,** where it lays on its **tummy** and pushes itself forward with its **wings.**

The **emperor penguin** is the world's **biggest** penguin. It is about as tall and weighs twice as much as an average 4-year-old child.

Emperor Penguin

This **huge** penguin is a **strong, fast swimmer**. It can **dive deeper** than any other **penguin**.

This penguin lives in **Antarctica**. Because it is so **cold** there, a **parent** penguin holds its **chick** on its feet to keep it **warm**.

Saltwater Crocodile

Saltwater crocodiles are the **biggest reptiles** in the world. They live in **rivers, swampy areas** and **estuaries**. They have also been seen **swimming in the ocean** far from land.

Crocodiles **don't sweat.** They **yawn** to cool down their **body temperature** quickly.

Biggest Reptile!

This huge croc can **leap straight up** to grab prey. It uses its **strong tail** to push its body out of the **water.**

Saltwater crocs have between **40** and **60** teeth. If one falls out, another tooth will **replace** it.

These crocodiles are also called **salties** and **estuarine crocodiles.**

Biggest Marsupial!

A **group** of kangaroos is called a **mob**.

Kangaroos are **good swimmers.** They **paddle** with their front paws and **kick** with their back legs. When swimming, they can **move** their back legs **one at a time.**

The red kangaroo is the biggest **marsupial** in the world. It lives in the **dry, sandy areas** of **central Australia.** An adult male can grow almost **as tall as a man.**

A kangaroo **cannot walk.** On land, the kangaroo can only move both **back legs** at the same time, so it has to **hop.**

Red kangaroos are most **active at night.** During the day they **laze** about in the **shade,** trying to keep **cool.**

Red kangaroo

Biggest Arthropod!

Japanese Spider Crab

The Japanese spider crab has a small body but really long legs. If you stretched them out, they would be as long as a car. It lives in the ocean around Japan.

This crab is a scavenger. It eats dead animals lying on the ocean floor. You can think of it as the vulture of the sea.

These crabs have 2 kinds of legs: walking legs and claw-bearing legs, called chelipeds. Many of these crabs seen in the wild are missing at least 1 leg. This may be because the legs get torn off by predators or caught in fishing nets. These crabs can live with as many as 3 walking legs missing. Walking legs may grow back when the crab moults.

The Publisher: KidsWorld Books

Library and Archives Canada Cataloguing in Publication

Giant animals / Einstein Sisters.

ISBN 978-0-9938401-3-5 (pbk.)

1. Body size—Juvenile literature. 2. Animals—Juvenile literature. I. Einstein Sisters, author

QL799.G52 2014   j591.4'1   C2014-904200-0

Cover Images: Front cover: Fuse/Thinkstock. *Back cover:* giraffe, sduben/Thinkstock; capybara, Viktor Cáp/Thinkstock; blue whale, Ian Sheldon.
Background Graphics: abstract background, Maryna Borysevych/Thinkstock, 5, 21, 31, 37, 63; pixels, Misko Kordic/Thinkstock, 6, 11, 14, 18, 22, 27, 28, 34, 37, 38, 43, 46, 48, 51, 54, 58, 61.
Photos Credits: Brent Barrett/Wikipedia, 47; Mnolf/Wikipedia, 46. Thinkstock: Anatoliy Fyodorov, 30; Andreas Altenburger, 62; Anup Shah, 35; Armin Rose, 56–57; bangkaewphoto, 38; Byrdyak, 60; Cepreih Uryadnihkov, 16–17; ChrisKrugerSA, 5; Christian Musat, 12, 21; cowboy5437, 52–53; demarfa, 54; Gerrit David de Vries, 6; hiansdown, 51; Jochen Kost, 31; johnnorth, 28; Josef Muellek, 63; Jupiterimages, 40–41; K_attapon, 19; Koonyongyut, 43; Maikab, 32–33; Maxim Pyshnyy, 42; mb-fotos, 61; MikeLane45, 26, 58; MR1805, 2–3; Nicolay Stanev, 59; OSTILL, 20; paulbcowell, 8–9; piyathep, 34; PrinPrince, 50; renacal1, 10; richcarey, 17; sduben, 7; Serge_Vero, 36; shalamov, 11; StuPorts, 4; tibu, 55; vencavolrab, 18; Viktor Cáp, 24–25; webguz, 44–45; Xiaoming Zhao, 48.

We acknowledge the financial support of the Government of Canada through the Canada Book Fund (CBF) for our publishing activities.

 Canadian   Patrimoine
Heritage   canadien

PC: 25